IT'S NOT MAGIC, It's Science!

IT'S NOT MAGIC, It's Science!

Hope Buttitta

Illustrated by
Tom LaBaff
&
Orrin Lundgren

50 Science Tricks that
MYSTIFY, DAZZLE & ASTOUND!

LARK BOOKS

A Division of Sterling Publishing Co., Inc.
New York

Editors
VERONIKA ALICE GUNTER
and JOE RHATIGAN

Creative Director,
Book Design, and Production
CELIA NARANJO

Illustrators
TOM LABAFF: pages 3, 5, 6, 7, 8,
9 (top and left), 10, 11, 12, 16, 18,
21, 23, 24, 28, 29, 32, 39, 42, 43, 47,
51, 54, 66, 68, 70, 76, and 77

ORRIN LUNDGREN: pages 9
(right), 14, 17, 22, 27, 30, 31, 35, 37,
40, 44, 45, 48, 49, 50, 53, 56, 57, 59,
62, 63, 64, 65, 67, 69, 71, 74, and 75

Cover Illustration
TOM LABAFF

Production Assistance
KRISTI PFEFFER

Editorial Assistance
DELORES GOSNELL and
SUSAN KIEFFER

Library of Congress Cataloging-in-Publication Data
Buttitta, Hope P.
   It's not magic, it's science! : 50 science tricks that mystify, dazzle &
astound / by Hope P. Buttitta.— 1st ed.
       p. cm.
   Includes index.
   ISBN 1-57990-622-2
   1. Science—Experiments. 2. Scientific recreations. I. Title.
Q164.B97 2004
793.8—dc22

                                                2004016518

10 9 8 7 6 5 4 3 2 1

First Edition

Published by Lark Books, a division of
Sterling Publishing Co., Inc.
387 Park Avenue South, New York, N.Y. 10016

© 2005, Hope Buttitta
Illustrations © Tom LaBaff, as indicated at left

Distributed in Canada by Sterling Publishing,
c/o Canadian Manda Group, 165 Dufferin Street
Toronto, Ontario, Canada M6K 3H6

Distributed in the U.K. by Guild of Master Craftsman Publications Ltd., Castle
Place, 166 High Street, Lewes, East Sussex, England BN7 1XU
Tel: (+ 44) 1273 477374, Fax: (+ 44) 1273 478606, e-mail: pubs@thegmc-
group.com, Web: www.gmcpublications.com

Distributed in Australia by Capricorn Link (Australia) Pty Ltd.,
P.O. Box 704, Windsor, NSW 2756 Australia

If you have questions or comments about this book, please contact:
Lark Books
67 Broadway
Asheville, NC 28801
(828) 253-0467

Manufactured in China

ISBN: 1-57990-622-2

7853

Acknowledgments

I'd like to thank the following people who made this book possible: my husband, Tim Buttitta, for his input and support during the countless hours I spent going over ideas; my son, Joseph, for occasionally napping so that I could work; my mother, Iris Pendergrass, for giving me the time away from motherhood to get the job done; my colleague and friend, Beth Snoke Harris, for sharing her wonderfully creative ideas; my editors, Veronika Alice Gunter and Joe Rhatigan, for giving me guidance and the opportunity to write this book; Tom LaBaff and Orrin Lundgren, for conveying the energy and fun of these science tricks with their watercolor illustrations; and creative director Celia Naranjo, who skillfully combined the fruits of our efforts on each page, creating the lively, engaging book you hold in your hands.

Contents

Lab Coat Magicians

Hi, I'm Tim. I love to wow my friends and family with amazing tricks—science tricks that are so unbelievable you'd think they're magic. It all started when my friends Lucinda and Jessie saw me practicing how to pick up a marble without touching it. (See page 35.) They started calling me Tim the Amazing—which I think is pretty cool. Now the three of us have collected more than 50 science tricks for you to use to impress your friends.

So what does magic have to do with science? A lot! Magicians create mysteries; scientists solve them. And a secret I've learned—this is something that not even smarty-pants Lucinda knew before I told her—is that magicians ARE scientists. They don't really make anything float or vanish in a puff of smoke. And they definitely can't break the laws of nature—they just make you think they do. To put on a good show, magicians need science know-how—

everything from physics and chemistry to physiology and psychology.

Some of these tricks sound impossible. Like seeing the hole in your hand that you never noticed before. (See page 61.) Magic? No. Your brain is fooled by mixed-up messages. And what about a no-sip straw? (See page 58.) Magic? Nope. You change the air pressure so no sipping or slurping can happen.

Most of these science tricks are great for showing off in front of an audience, like overpowering a person with just your pinky. (See page 28.) Sure, it looks like you have super powers, but it's an easy trick when you have gravity on your side!

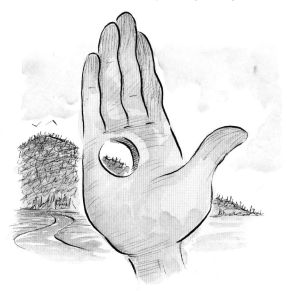

My favorite trick is making an egg squeeze itself into a tight space. How? Turn to page 19 to find out.

These tricks work because of science, from Newton's laws of motion and Bernoulli's principles about fluids to simple electricity, and more. So after you amaze your audience with the magic, you can triple wow them with the science. You'll read about it in the "How It Works" section after each set of instructions. We also reveal secret magician techniques, science history, and more.

Since it looks strange to see a magician wearing a lab coat (just look at Lucinda!), most scientists who perform their tricks dress up and act out a fun personality. (We are Tim the Amazing, Jessie the Great, and Lucinda the Splendiferous.)

Let's get started with these dazzling and astounding tricks. Thanks for coming to the show!

Using This Book

Want to balance objects like a master magician? Make water disappear without drinking it? Transform a straw into a knife? You can. The secrets to these and other remarkable acts that defy explanation are at the tips of your fingers right now.

How to Do the Tricks

You can test and perform most of these tricks on your own. You don't have to know anything about science or magic to begin. You do need to read everything about each trick before you try it. Then gather the stuff needed and follow the instructions. Every now and then you'll need to get an adult to give you a hand. We'll tell you when. Don't skip that part.

Let's look at how to make your science tricks go smoothly:

1   Gather all your materials in one place, making sure not to leave out or substitute anything.

2   Carefully read through the instructions and the explanation to make sure you understand what you'll be doing.

3   You'll need a flat surface for most of these tricks. A kitchen table makes a good work area because you can stand behind it to perform your trick. Make sure to clear it off before you begin and clean up when you're finished.

4 Practice, practice, practice. This is the fun part. Practice the trick several times by yourself before you show it to your audience. Realize that the trick may not work perfectly every time. Even magicians, professional science educators, and scientists have things go wrong when performing demonstrations.

5 During the trick, don't give the answer away. Let the audience try to figure out what's going on. Wait until they've made several attempts to solve the mystery of the trick and then give them the explanation if you want. Guessing how you did the trick is half the fun.

6 Clean up! All solid materials in this book can be disposed of in your garbage can at home or, if liquid, in the sink drain with plenty of water.

Before the Big Show

Most of these science tricks are great for showing off to an audience, like balancing a spinning penny and making a cup cackle. So, after you've practiced, practiced, and practiced some more, why not gather friends and family to witness your best tricks?

Think about which science tricks you'll do and how many people you'd like to invite. Then choose a space that offers enough room for everyone, plus the tables, chairs, or other things you'll need.

If possible, choose a space that feels just right for a magic show. Jessie uses her kitchen. Lucinda prefers to do everything in her garage laboratory. I use the porch at my house. I feel as if I am up on a real stage, and there's plenty of room for my audience in the front yard.

Wherever you choose to perform, you need to practice the tricks in this space, even after you've practiced them elsewhere.

When I'm doing these tricks I like to wear a costume and be in character. I'll even have my Mom or Dad be the stage announcer and introduce me—as Tim the Amazing, of course.

It all makes the show more fun for me, and I think the audience likes it, too. Whether or not you put on a costume or change your name is up to you. If you do, practice in the costume so you are comfortable. Make sure that no part of it gets in the way of the trick or makes you trip or fall.

Sometimes we use specialized science and magic words in the instructions. If they are new to you, look up their definitions in the glossary on page 78. (Anytime we use a word that's in the glossary, we'll put it in **bold**.)

The Big Show

Ready? Be confident. Have fun. Doing science tricks and illusions is easy. It's just a matter of playing on science rules about gravity, air pressure, motion, force, optics, and more.

The show will go smoothly if you practice good showmanship. That means getting the audience to pay attention and care about how the trick will turn out, and doing the trick well enough so the audience doesn't figure out how it works. (That's why you practiced it so many times.)

We'll explain the science behind each trick. You decide if you want to share it with the audience after the show, or if you want to repeat the trick until they figure it out.

Never, ever, reveal the secrets to another person's trick while she's performing it. That violates the code of conduct for magicians everywhere. And just think of how it would make you feel if it happened to you!

Go For It!

When it comes to making the impossible possible, it's science, not magic, that does the trick. With just a little bit of practice you'll soon be amazing your friends and family with what you learn. Have fun!

Common Sense Tips

You really need to read this section. It's short but important.

- Read each trick (every word!) before trying it. Then collect what you need and choose the spot that will serve as your practice or performance space. Get an adult's permission for wherever you choose.

- If something unfamiliar is on a What You Need list, ask an adult to help you find it. You might need to visit a drug store or a supermarket.

- Don't use the supplies or materials for anything besides what is instructed.

- Wash your hands very well after handling any substances— even if you didn't spill any.

- Use clean containers (jars, cups, glasses, bowls) for your tricks. You can sometimes substitute containers or vary their sizes. Collect recyclables, such as empty jars, to substitute for drinking glasses.

- If you make a mess, clean it up.

- Get an adult to help you whenever there's a heat source involved, or anything using a flame.

- If you aren't sure what to do or have questions, stop what you are doing and find an adult for help.

The Balancing Bottles

Practice makes perfect if you want to "pull off" this trick.

What You Need

- 2 glass soda bottles
- Flat surface or table
- Dollar bill

What You Do

1. Tell your audience that after you perform this trick you'll invite them each to try and whomever gets it right on the first try can keep the dollar.

2. Put one glass soda bottle on the table. Place one end of the dollar bill on top of the bottle's mouth so that most of the dollar bill hangs down.

3. Balance the second bottle upside down on top of the first bottle, with the dollar bill sandwiched between their mouths. It may take several tries to balance them. You're now ready to begin your trick.

4. Hold the dollar bill with one hand and steady the bottle on top with the other hand.

5. Let go of the bottle and quickly jerk the dollar bill from between the bottles. The dollar bill should slide out without knocking the bottles over. Now let the audience try!

6. You may have to practice several times before showing off this trick. Don't give up! If you move the dollar bill too slowly, it causes the bottles to be pulled along with the dollar bill.

More Balancing Fun

When you get really good at this, find a thin, silky tablecloth or piece of fabric and put it on a table. Place dishes or cups on top of the table. Firmly grasp the edge of the fabric with both hands and pull quickly. The dishes should remain on the table while the cloth slides out from beneath them. Once you're an expert at this you can add water to some of the cups and try not to spill.

How It Works

Isaac Newton was a scientist who studied how things move or stay where they are. In these tricks, the objects stay at rest (don't move) while the dollar bill or table-cloth moves. Newton said that objects at **rest** remain at rest unless they are acted upon by a **force** (like your hand knocking them over). He also said objects in **motion** remain in motion unless a force acts upon them. (The dollar bill moves until you stop moving your hand.) Why does pulling the dollar bill quickly help? That way there's no time for friction (resistance between moving objects) to develop.

The Great Phone Book Strength Test

Don't giggle at your volunteers' feeble attempts to perform this feat. (Only you know it's impossible!)

What You Need
- 2 volunteers
- 2 phone books of the same size (the larger, the better)
- Tabletop

What You Do

1. Before you begin, have a volunteer flip through the pages of each phone book to demonstrate that they are ordinary phone books.

2. Shuffle the phone book pages together as you would a deck of cards, so that the pages overlap each other about halfway. Place the two books that you have shuffled on a table.

3. Ask a volunteer to separate the two by pulling them apart. When he struggles, ask him to pull as hard as he can.

4. Ask someone else to help, so that there is one person holding each phone book. They won't be able to pull them apart!

How It Works

When a leaning pile of papers begins to fall off a desk, each paper slides easily and glides to the floor. That's because there's very little **friction.** In this trick, the phone book pages are piled upon one another. It's the combined weight of each of the phone book pages, one on top of the other, that creates an enormous amount of friction—enough to hold the books together.

Magnetic Water

What You Need
- Water
- Large glass
- Index card
- Trashcan or bucket

Masters of this trick perform it over a volunteer's head. (I say begin over a bucket, unless you've got friends to spare.)

What You Do

1 Perform this science trick over a trashcan or empty bucket, just in case. Fill the glass about three-quarters full with water. Tell your audience that you can turn this glass of water upside down without spilling it—using only an index card!

2 Show them the index card. Place the index card on top of the glass so that it fully covers it. Hold the card on top with your palm.

3 With your other hand, quickly turn the glass of water upside down. Remove your hand from the card. The water will stay in the glass until the paper becomes saturated and starts to leak.

How It Works

In addition to water, there's air in the glass. Both have **pressure.** The air outside the glass, however, has a greater pressure than the water inside, and will push against the index card, holding the water in. The card will eventually weaken as it soaks up water and breaks the **seal.** How strong is this pressure? You would get the same results even if the column of water was 30 feet tall.

Eggs With Legs

Okay, the eggs won't actually grow legs, but they will jump around a bit.

What You Need

- Large egg
- 2 very short glasses with a mouth that the egg can sit in (Shot glasses work well—ask your parents for these.)

What You Do

1. When you perform this, tell your audience you will move the egg from one glass to the other without touching the egg. But practice it several times before performing it. Plan on breaking a few eggs during practice!

2. Place the two glasses so that one is in front of the other and they are touching.

3. Put the egg in the glass nearest you.

4. Blow as hard as you can towards the egg. The egg should leap out of the glass and into the next one!

How It Works

Something called the **Bernoulli effect** is taking place here. The air you blow toward the egg hits the egg and then goes up and over it. This creates an area of low **pressure** above the egg. Meanwhile, the air below the egg has a higher pressure. This causes the egg to lift out of the glass. If you just blow softly, this trick will not work because the air above the egg has to be moving faster than the air below it. (See pages 41-43 for more about the Bernoulli effect.)

In-egg-splicable

This hard-boiled science trick will have your audience scratching their heads in disbelief.

What You Need

- Adult helper
- Hard-boiled egg
- Glass bottle with opening slightly smaller than egg (apple cider or juice bottles work well)
- Matches

What You Do

1 Have the adult helper hard-boil an egg. Note: You may want to hard-boil several eggs at a time to do the trick more than once. Remove the pot from the stove and place the pot and egg under cold running water for a few minutes. Let the egg cool.

2 Remove the egg from the water and peel the shell. Then gather an audience.

3 Place the egg on the opening of the bottle to show your audience that the egg will not simply fall into the bottle. Tell your audience you can get this egg to go into the bottle in one piece.

4 Have the adult light two matches and quickly drop them into the bottle. Quickly place the egg on top of the bottle, wait a few seconds, and watch your egg drop into the bottle.

How It Works

When you drop matches into the bottle, the air heats up. As the heated air **expands**, some of it comes out of the bottle. When the match flames go out, the air inside the bottle cools and **contracts**. The egg on the bottle creates a **seal**. The **pressure** inside the bottle is now less than the pressure outside the bottle and, since nature prefers things to be equal, the egg is forced into the bottle. To get the egg out of the bottle, heat the bottle or blow into it. The increased air pressure will force the egg back out.

19

Eggs of Steel

The egg's amazing structure makes it perfect for magic and science tricks. The curved shape gives it great strength. It resembles an architectural dome. A dome is able to support weight from the top by spreading the weight out along the entire dome. A dome absorbs force the same way: the force radiates throughout the dome, lessening the force's impact. Domes have been used in building for centuries, since at least the famous Pantheon in Rome, built in 27 BCE. (Which makes you wonder: Did architects look at the egg for design tips?)

The shape explains why an egg can withstand compression (like squeezing it in your hand) without breaking. (Try this! Evenly apply the pressure.) It can also withstand a large amount of force on its top and bottom, which is what happens when an egg falls from the hen to the ground.

Eggs aren't indestructible, though. The shell's material, calcium carbonate, is strong enough to withstand a mother hen sitting on top of it, but thin enough for a chick to break out of it with its sharp beak. Also, when you put pressure across just the middle, an egg will easily break. That's why most folks crack the center of an egg against the edge of a bowl or frying pan to open it.

You can dazzle an audience with an egg's fragility or toughness, depending on how you handle it. Cut four egg holders from an egg carton. Place an egg in each holder. Place a book on top of the eggs with one egg under each corner of the book. How many books can you stack on top without breaking the eggs? You might be surprised!

Won't Do It, Can't Make Me

What You Need

- Volunteer
- Plastic drink bottle
- Small piece of paper

Watch an itty-bitty piece of paper with a mind of its own vex a volunteer.

What You Do

1. Remove the paper label from the drink bottle so that you can easily see inside the bottle. Ball up the piece of paper so that it will fit inside the mouth of the bottle.

2. Hold the bottle horizontally with the piece of paper sitting in the mouth of the bottle near the edge.

3. Ask a volunteer to try to blow the paper into the bottle. The paper will jump out!

Blow Hards Wanted

How It Works

Even though you can't see it, the bottle is filled with air. When you blow on the paper, the air in the bottle is pushing back through the mouth of the bottle. A puff of breath is not strong enough to force the paper inside.

Air Cannon

Just a tap of your fingertips launches a whirling blast of air.

What You Need

- Adult helper
- Plastic milk jug (without the lid)
- Scissors
- Large self-closing plastic bag
- Strong tape such as duct or packaging tape
- Candle with holder
- Matches

What You Do

1. Have the adult cut out the bottom of the milk jug with the scissors.

2. Cut one side and the bottom of the plastic bag. Open it so that you have a large piece of plastic.

3. Stretch the plastic over the hole you have made in the milk jug.

4. Securely tape the plastic to the sides of the jug so that there are no holes for air to escape.

5. Assemble an audience and then light the candle. Tell your audience you can extinguish the candle's flame without using your breath or touching it. Move about a yard away. (You'll be able to increase the distance with practice.)

6. Aim the jug so that the mouth is facing toward the candle. With your hand, firmly tap the plastic-covered hole. Air will shoot out of the cannon, blowing out your candle's flame.

22

FUN with Vortex Generators

With what!? The contraption you made for this trick is a homemade version of what scientists call a **vortex generator**. It creates a wave of air shaped like a flat ring. (That's the **vortex**.) The air at the center of the mouth of the bottle is moving faster than the air around the sides so as you compress air out of the jug, the mouth creates a donut-shaped ring of air. Here are some ideas for more vortex generating contraptions:

• Make air cannons out of water bottles, soup cans, 5-gallon buckets, or even plastic trashcans. You can use balloons, plastic garbage bags, or plastic tarps to cover the bottom of your air container. Increase the distance from the candle as you increase the size of your cannon.

• Aim your cannon at a small pool of water. You will see the vortex or rings that it creates in the water.

• You can make a smoke cannon using the same objects. Have an adult help you use a stick of incense to create smoke. Carefully place the lit incense stick inside the open end of the cannon. Once a good amount of smoke has collected, take the stick out and fire away!

How It Works

Air occupies space. When you tap the plastic on the jug's bottom, air is forced out of the mouth. That's because as the plastic is pushed toward the inside of the jug, the space inside gets smaller and forces some air out of the hole. The harder you tap, the more air you'll force out. The smaller the mouth of the jug, the faster the air comes out.

23

Light-headed

The secret to this trick will leave your audience breathless—and maybe even dizzy.

What You Need

- 2 volunteers
- 2 plastic drink bottles (20-ounce or 1-liter bottles work well)
- Thumbtack
- Several latex balloons

What You Do

1. Before performing the trick, use the thumbtack to make a small hole in the bottom of one of the plastic bottles. The hole should be about the size of a small nail head. It needs to be big enough for air to come out but small enough that you can't easily see it.

2. Gather you audience and pick two volunteers. Tell them you're having a contest to see who can blow up a balloon in a bottle the fastest. Ask the volunteers to blow up balloons at the same time. This is to show everyone else they can blow up a balloon outside of a bottle.

3. For the "contest," give one volunteer the bottle with the hole, but don't tell her about the hole. Give the other volunteer the bottle without the hole.

4. Ask the volunteers to place a deflated balloon inside the bottle so that the balloon opening is stretched over the mouth of the bottle. On the count of three, ask both volunteers to blow up their balloon. The person without the hole in their bottle will not be able to do it!

5. Take the bottle with the hole in it from your volunteer, secretly put your finger over the hole, and ask the other volunteer to try this one. Replace the balloon with a new one, to avoid sharing germs. Don't take your finger from the hole. Watch frustration set in. Ask other volunteers to try while your finger is either on or off the hole. (Give each new volunteer a clean balloon.) Only show your audience the hole if you want to.

How It Works

Air is taking up space in both bottles. In the bottle without the hole, the volunteer is trying to move the air or **compress** it just by blowing. This is very difficult to do because the **pressure** from the air inside pushing back at the balloon is greater than the air pressure created by blowing. With a hole in the bottom of the other bottle, the air is compressed as the balloon **inflates** and air can escape from the bottle. For more fun, place your finger over the hole once the balloon is inflated and stop blowing into the bottle. The balloon will stay inflated. This is because the air can no longer escape from the hole. Now the air pressure inside the balloon is greater than the air pressure inside the bottle.

Is the Hand Quicker Than the Eye?

Sleight of hand can describe anything you do so quickly and carefully that no one notices what you've done. From sneaking a bite of your dad's dessert to covering a secret hole (see Light-headed on page 24) or putting your thumb in just the right spot to pierce an apple (see Sharp as a Knife on page 36), that's sleight of hand.

Does that mean the hand is quicker than the eye? Not at all! It takes much longer for a thought to travel through your nervous system and activate the muscles in your hand than it does to get a similar message to your eyes. Test it: Can you look to the top of this page quicker than you can touch it?

Good performers (and mischievous kids) know that the eye is quicker—but they also know that the eye can be fooled. You just have to combine **physical feats** and **showmanship**. First, practice the trick in front of a mirror until you do it perfectly. For instance, in Magic Hand on page 55 you conceal a tablet in your hand. (The trick is much more fun to perform when you keep the tablet a secret, so practice it.) Then, when performing whichever trick you've mastered, **misdirect** the audience's attention with magician's **patter**—talk that's meant to entertain and take their minds off figuring out the trick. (Remember, you can't move faster than their eyes.) In Light-headed, you exaggerate your surprise when the balloon does not inflate and you let other people try. In Magic Hand, you talk about your hand and wave it around, so the audience isn't looking for a secret ingredient in the other hand. Whenever you take your audience's mind off figuring out the trick, you can really wow them.

Boiling Ice

What You Need

- Adult helper
- Glass test tube (Ask to borrow one from your science teacher or order one from a science supply store.)
- Crushed ice
- Steel wool (can be purchased at the grocery or hardware store)
- Water
- Metal tongs or test tube holder
- Candle lighter

What You Do

1 Begin by filling the test tube about one-third full with crushed ice. Pull out a small amount of steel wool from the pad and put it on top of the ice. Press it firmly into the tube. Fill the test tube with cold water.

2 Have an adult light the candle lighter and, with the tongs, hold the middle portion of the test tube over the flame.

3 Heat the water until it boils. The ice will not melt.

How It Works

If the ice was allowed to float in the water and then the water was heated, the ice would **melt** due to **convection**. This means that as the water warms it would rise because it's less **dense** and it would melt the icy water at the top. In this trick, however, the ice is held at the bottom of the test tube by the steel wool. The cold water in the top of the test tube warms when heated—and even boils—and becomes less dense. But it's already on top and doesn't circulate to the bottom.

Pinky Power

Your littlest finger is the unlikely conqueror that unbalances a volunteer of any size.

What You Need
- Volunteer
- Chair

What You Do

1   Gather an audience and tell them that you will demonstrate the previously unrevealed power of a pinky. Ask a volunteer to sit all the way back in the chair with his hands in his lap. Point and place your pinky finger in the center of his forehead.

2   Ask him to stand up without using his hands or arms to help. He can't do it!

How It Works

The **center of gravity**, also known as the **center of mass**, is a point where most of the object's **mass** is concentrated. For humans, if your center of mass is not over your base of support (like a chair or your feet) you will lose your **balance**. You can find the center of mass of any object by balancing it on your finger (assuming it's not a refrigerator!). The point where it balances is its center of mass. In this trick, in order to stand from a seated position you must lean forward to move your center of mass over your feet (the base of support). If a pinky is there to prevent that shift, you can't stand up.

Chair Lift

Flabbergast your friends by correctly predicting who can and who can't perform a seemingly simple feat.

What You Need

- Boy and girl volunteers
- Chair
- Wall

What You Do

1 Place the chair next to the wall and turn it sideways. Without making it obvious that you are choosing one boy and one girl, say you need volunteers for a pretty simple task. Ask a boy to stand beside the chair and face the wall. He should be about two foot-lengths from the wall. Make sure his feet are not under the chair.

2 Tell him to lean over the chair and place his head against the wall with his back flat. Ask him to try to pick up the chair and then stand up with it without moving his feet or bending his knees. (Most likely he won't be able to do this.) Say you knew he couldn't do it, but thank him for trying.

3 Say you know who can do it, and ask for a girl volunteer to give it a try. Most likely she will be able to do it.

How It Works

The **center of mass** for boys and men is higher in their bodies than for girls and women. When a boy bends over the chair his mass is centered over the chair instead of over his feet, so he cannot perform this task without losing his **balance**. A girl's center of mass is closer to her hips and over her feet when she tries to lift the chair, so she can stand up and not lose her balance.

BaLLooN Kebabs

No, this isn't what clowns eat at clown barbecues. It's a trick that takes the "pop" out of piercing a balloon.

What You Need
- Several latex balloons
- Bamboo skewers (available at grocery stores)
- Cooking oil

What You Do

1. Blow up the balloon about three-quarters full, so that there is still some room for air. Tie it off with a knot. Dip the sharp end of a bamboo skewer into some cooking oil.

2. Assemble an audience. Tell them you can put the skewer through the balloon without popping it. Find a spot near the knot of the inflated balloon where the latex is thicker and darker than the rest of the balloon. Using the sharp end of the skewer, gently twist it around and around while pushing it through the balloon.

3. Once the skewer is in the balloon on one side, twist and push the skewer through the opposite side of the balloon (near the top). It will come out the other side without popping the balloon. Note: The balloon will slowly deflate as the air leaks out, but this can take a while. See how many skewers you can put through one balloon!

How It Works

Balloons are made of thin sheets of rubber latex. Latex is made up of molecules called **polymers**, which are in large **strands**. These strands of molecules are stretchy, which is why you can blow up a balloon. When you don't blow it up fully, some of the polymer strands are not stretched to their maximum at places, like at the knot or top of the balloon. So, when you puncture the balloon with the skewer at those spots, the polymer strands can stretch around the skewer without popping the balloon.

Balloon First-Aid

What You Need

- Round latex balloon
- Penny
- Cooking oil
- Needle or straight pin

What You Do

1. Put a penny inside the balloon. Blow up the balloon so that it's not fully inflated and tie it off.

2. Hold the balloon with the tied end in your palm. Swirl it around and around by moving your hand back and forth. The penny will orbit inside. This is pretty cool already, but there's more.

3. Dip the end of the needle in the oil to lubricate it. Gently twist the needle into the thickest part of the balloon, the area opposite the knot, to make a small hole. Remove the needle.

4. Again, orbit the penny inside the balloon by moving your hand back and forth. When the penny slows down, allow it to come to rest over the hole. Turn the balloon so that it is right-side up, with the hole on top. The penny will stay in place, patching the hole.

How It Works

When you blow up the balloon, the air inside is **compressed** and has more **pressure** than the air outside the balloon. The air pushes on the penny to keep it in place, sealing the hole and keeping the balloon **inflated**.

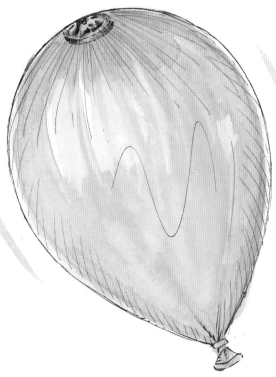

Bed of Nails

Here's one bed you don't want to wake up in.

What You Need

- Adult helper
- Two pieces of 10 x 10-inch plywood
- Hammer
- Aluminum gutter nails
- Several large balloons
- Several heavy books

What You Do

1 Have an adult help you hammer the nails into one piece of the plywood. Each nail should be about 1 inch from the next and stick out the other side of the plywood.

2 Blow up two balloons so that they're filled to half their maximum size, and tie them off.

3 When you're ready to perform, assemble an audience and tell them that you will lay a balloon on a bed of nails without popping it. To prove that the nails are real, put one balloon on just one nail and press down on it to pop the balloon.

4 Lay the bed of nails on a flat surface and place a balloon filled with air on top.

5 Place the second piece of plywood on top of the balloon. You may need to steady it with your hands. Place one book at a time on the plywood. The balloon will not pop!

6 Continue to add books to see how many it takes to eventually pop the balloon.

How It Works

When the balloon is placed on one nail and a small amount of **force** is added (your hand), the **pressure** is enough to pop the balloon because it is applied to such a small area (one spot on the balloon's surface). When the balloon is placed on the bed of nails, however, the pressure from the nails is distributed over a large area and the balloon doesn't pop. Even when you add more weight, the balloon stays **inflated** as long as the weight is distributed over the whole balloon. The pressure that is applied is equal to the amount of force divided by the area ($P = F/A$). So, if the area is increased, and you use the same amount of force (the piece of plywood on top), less pressure is created on each individual point.

More Fun

Place a polystyrene foam cup upside down and try to stand on it. It will crush under the pressure. Now, stack several polystyrene foam cups upside down and very close together. Place a thin board on top and stand on it. The pressure you put on each cup is decreased and spread out over the total number of cups, therefore it can hold you.

Napping on Nails, Walking on Fire

Traveling **conjurers** invented the Bed of Nails trick in India a thousand years ago. They used their own bodies in place of the balloon, but the science is the same.

These con artists pretended to be monks called **fakirs**. They performed "miracles," such as lying on beds of nails, fire walking, and eating fire. They weren't trying to entertain their audiences with cool magic tricks—they scared people out of their money by claiming to have supernatural powers. Even the poorest people gave these con artists money so they'd leave their village in peace. (I know I'd do just about anything to get a fire-eater out of my neighborhood!)

Sure, some of these tricks may make you look like you have supernatural powers, but it's not magic—it's science! You know the science behind Bed of Nails (see page 32). Eating fire is actually done by extinguishing a fire in your mouth. Fire needs oxygen, and flames go up in search of oxygen. Performers tilt their heads back just right so the flame and heat stay on the wick instead of touching their mouths. Fire-eaters can cut off the supply of oxygen by closing their mouths or exhaling. Fire walking relies on the fact that something that is very hot doesn't necessarily release a lot of heat. Firewalkers step on burning coals because the coals are good insulators (they retain heat). Firewalkers walk quickly, taking about a quarter second per step, so there's not time for their feet to get hot and burn. These tricks are dangerous, but there's nothing supernatural about them. (Do not try them.)

When the fake fakirs performed their tricks in front of good scientific thinkers, their sham was revealed. (Maybe that's why we call a person who pretends to be something he isn't a "faker.")

Simply Marble-ous

Your audience might ask you if you've lost your marbles when you offer to pick up one in a bottomless cup.

What You Need
- Paper cup
- Scissors
- Marbles (more than one in case you lose some!)
- Tabletop

What You Do

1 Cut the bottom out of the paper cup. Make sure the edges are smooth. Place a marble on the table and gather an audience. Show them the cup. Tell your audience that you can put the marble into the cup without touching the marble.

2 Place the cup over the marble so that the bottom of the cup is resting on the tabletop. Holding the cup in your hand, rotate it in a small circular motion on the table. Don't lift the cup off the table. The marble should be rotating with the cup.

3 Once the marble is rotating quickly, slowly lift the cup off the table while continuing to rotate the cup. The marble will continue to spin inside the cup.

How It Works

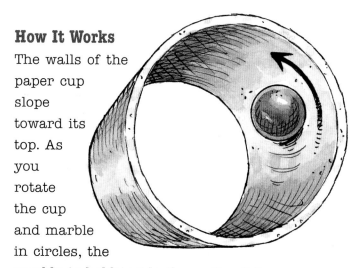

The walls of the paper cup slope toward its top. As you rotate the cup and marble in circles, the marble is held inside the walls of the cup because of **centripetal force**. That is, the marble wants to go in a straight line but the walls of the cup force it to go in a circle. It then travels up the sides of the cup because of its **inertia,** or tendency to remain in **motion**, and pushes against the walls of the cup. If you rotate the cup too slowly, the marble will fall out and fly across the room.

Sharp as a Knife

Let your friends try this trick first. Then they'll really be astonished when you succeed!

What You Need

- Volunteers
- Plastic drinking straws (not the flexible type)
- Apple

What You Do

1. Gather an audience. Tell them you can pierce the apple with a measly straw. Invite volunteers to try to "stab" the apple themselves. Once they give up, hold the apple with your fingers on the top and bottom. This is so that when you punch the straw through, you won't hit your hand.

2. Cover one opening of the straw with your other thumb. Thrust the straw into the apple. It will go through as if it were a knife!

How It Works

When you close one opening of the straw, the air cannot escape from that end. As the straw hits the apple skin, the other opening closes and traps the air inside the straw. This makes the straw very rigid and increases the air **pressure** inside. With very little **force**, the straw goes through the apple.

The Big Bounce

Raise some eyebrows by making a flat basketball bounce.

What You Need

- Large, open space
- Semi-deflated basketball
- Large rubber ball such as a volleyball or four-square ball

What You Do

1. Try to bounce the basketball to show that it will barely get off the ground. In this trick you'll make the ball bounce without refilling it with air.

2. Place the basketball on top of the large rubber ball and hold them in the air.

3. Let go of the balls at the same time. The bottom ball will bounce and send the basketball flying!

How It Works

The **energy** from the bottom ball hitting the ground and bouncing is transferred to the ball on the top and sends it flying. This is similar to a game of pool. When you strike the cue ball, it has energy. It hits another ball and transfers the energy, sending it across the pool table. This is because of Newton's **laws of motion** (see page 52).

More Fun

Try this with other types of balls—ping-pong, small rubber ones, large ones, more than two, etc. Try balls made of hard materials such as golf balls and baseballs, but please do this trick outside and away from other people and car windows. The balls can really fly!

Soda Squirt

Do this trick with a bunch of friends who aren't afraid of getting a little wet and sticky.

What You Need

- Volunteers
- Cans of unopened carbonated beverages (not "diet" soda)
- Outdoor location

What You Do

1. Gather your volunteers in a circle outdoors. Have each volunteer take a can of soda and shake it. Make sure they shake it a lot.

2. Tell them to open their cans close to their faces on the count of "three." You might also want to mention that even though you've shaken your can just as much as they have, you're not going to get wet.

3. Start your countdown, and right before opening your can, tap the side of the can three times with your index finger. Open your can along with everyone else and watch as everyone else gets soaked while you stay dry.

How It Works

Carbon dioxide gas is dissolved into soda to make it bubbly and as a preservative to make it last longer. To get the gas into the can, it must be pressurized. That means the **pressure** inside the can is greater than outside the can. Opening the can depressurizes the soda, and the gas escapes in the form of bubbles. Shaking a can of soda agitates the gas and makes bubbles form on the insides of the can. If you had opened the can immediately after shaking it, you would have released the pressure and forced the bubbles out of the can, along with the soda blocking their path! Tapping on the side of the can causes all the bubbles to rise to the top. When you open the can, very little liquid is below the bubbles, so the gas can escape without forcing the soda out with it.

Can Crusher

What You Need

- Adult helper
- Water
- Measuring spoons
- Empty aluminum drink can
- Gas stovetop
- Oven mitts
- Metal tongs
- Clear bowl of water

What You Do

1. Place about 2 tablespoons of water into the can.

2. With an adult nearby, turn on the gas stovetop. Put on the oven mitts. With the metal tongs, hold the can over the flame, but not in the flame. You may smell some paint burning off the can.

3. When you see steam coming out of the can, quickly turn it upside down in the bowl of water so that just the top of the can touches the top of the water. This will create a seal.

4. Within a few seconds you should see and hear the can crush.

Who needs brute strength when you can crush a can with some water and a little heat?

How It Works

Even though you can't see it, air is all around us—and it has weight. This weight creates what is called air **pressure**, and at sea level this pressure equals about 15 pounds per square inch. In this science trick, air inside the can has pressure before we heat it that's equal to the pressure outside the can. When you place the can over the open flame, the water in the can begins to boil and creates steam. As the steam rises and exits the opening of the can, some air goes with it. When you turn the can upside down on the bowl of water, you create a **seal** to stop the air from leaving the can. As the air and water vapor left in the can cool, the air pressure inside the can decreases and the air outside the can crushes the can.

40

The Science of Flying and Floating

Scientific principles explain why things fly and float—from airplanes to round cheese puffs. Daniel Bernoulli was a Swiss scientist and mathematician who figured some of this out.

He lived in the 1700s and was interested in **fluid** and **pressure**. So he punctured the wall of a pipe carrying fluid with an open-ended straw. He noticed that the height of the fluid up the straw was related to its pressure in the pipe. He then developed a method of measuring blood pressure in humans using a glass tube in an artery. A similar tube was later used to measure air speed in airplanes.

Bernoulli is probably most famous for his fluid principle, often referred to as the "Bernoulli principle." It says that as the speed of a fluid (water, air, oil, etc.) increases, its pressure decreases. (Air is considered a fluid, but not a liquid. Anything that flows is a fluid. Therefore all gases are fluids.)

This principle is used when designing the wings of aircraft. The air moving over the curved surface of the top of the wing moves faster than the air beneath the wing, so the pressure is greater underneath. This causes the wing to lift upward.

Often when you see something fly or float, the Bernoulli principle is at work. Turn the page to find three science tricks that demonstrate this principle.

Up, Down, and All Around

Air is the invisible hand that helps you perform these tricks.

Wind Spin

What You Need
- Roll of toilet paper
- Plunger or broom
- Hairdryer

What You Do

1 Place the roll of toilet paper on the plunger handle so it can spin freely. Hold the plunger horizontally while you blow air from the hair dryer across the top of the roll of toilet paper. Look out! The roll will spin and the paper will come flying off.

How It Works

The air beneath the toilet paper has a higher pressure than that on top, so the toilet paper goes flying. It's the **Bernoulli principle** at work. (See page 41.)

Floating Cheese Puff

What You Need

- Flexible plastic straw
- Round cheese puff (from your favorite snack bag)

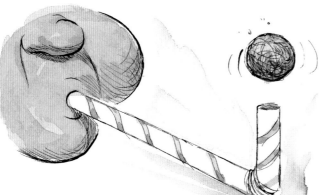

What You Do

1 Place the straight end of the straw into your mouth with the flexible end bent upright.

2 Hold the cheese puff just above the bent end of the straw. Blow. The cheese puff will float and balance on the stream of air.

How It Works

As you blow through the straw, the fast moving air creates less **pressure** around the puff than the surrounding air. The greater pressure keeps the puff in your airstream. Even if the puff tried to fall out of the stream, it would be pushed back in.

When Up Means Down

What You Need

- Paper
- Scissors

What You Do

1 Cut a strip of paper about 2 inches wide and 6 inches long.

2 Hold one end of the paper near your mouth and blow across the top of the paper. Instead of blowing the paper down, the paper will lift up.

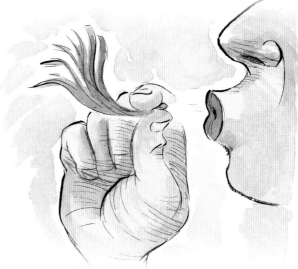

How It Works

The paper gets an upward lift like an airplane wing, thanks to the **Bernoulli principle**. Blowing across the top of the paper decreases pressure on top. With more pressure underneath, the paper lifts up.

The Cackling Cup

Hah Hee Har

In this trick you're going to tell a joke so bad that only a paper cup will laugh.

What You Need

- 2 paper clips
- Small paper cup
- Cotton string
- Scissors
- Glass of water
- A bad joke

What You Do

1 Open a paper clip and use one end to make a small hole in the bottom of the cup.

2 Cut a 12-inch piece of string. Tie one end of the string to the other paper clip.

3 Insert the other end of the string through the hole in the cup. Pull it through so that the paper clip rests on the inside bottom of the cup.

4 Assemble an audience and tell them you can make this paper cup laugh. Wet the string by dipping it into the glass of water. Hold the cup in one hand. Firmly grasp the string between the thumb and forefinger of your other hand where the string comes out.

5 Tell your horrible joke, and slide your fingers up the string making a "pull, stop, pull, stop" motion. Your cup should be the only thing or person laughing out loud.

6 Try using different types of cups, aluminum cans, etc. and different types of string to make new laugh makers. How many different guffaws can you produce?

How It Works

When the wet string is pulled, it begins to **vibrate**. This causes the paper clip to also vibrate. These vibrations form **sound waves** inside the cup that bounce off the walls of the cup. The sound is concentrated and amplified by the shape of the cup.

One Tough Toothpick

Challenge a big, strong member of your audience to break a wooden toothpick... but he must follow your directions on how to do it.

What You Need
- 2 volunteers
- Wooden toothpicks

What You Do

1. Place a toothpick horizontally on top of your strong volunteer's middle finger. Put his first and third fingers on top of either side of the toothpick.

2. Slide the toothpick down to the end of his fingers just below the nails. Ask the volunteer to try to break the toothpick using his first and third fingers. Guess what, he can't do it.

3. Ask a smaller person to give it a try. (A younger sibling should work nicely.) This time, slide it up toward his knuckles and ask the new volunteer to break the toothpick using his first and third fingers. This time your volunteer should be able to break the toothpick.

How It Works

The fingers act as a **lever**. Levers are simple machines that help us perform work with less **effort** and **force**. Some examples of levers are scissors, can openers, and wrenches. Levers have a pivot point called the **fulcrum**. The joint or knuckle is the fulcrum in this trick. Where you place the load (the thing you're trying to lift or break) and where you apply force can make all the difference. With the toothpick at the end of your fingers, it's almost impossible to break it. This is because the fulcrum is too far away from where you're applying force. When you slide the toothpick closer to the fulcrum, the task becomes easier because less force is needed.

Hot or Cold?

What You Need

- 2 volunteers
- Table
- 3 bowls
- Water
- Watch or clock

You'll get a warm reaction when you perform this cool trick.

What You Do

1. Pour cold water into one bowl. Pour hot tap water into the other. Make sure the hot water is not too hot; you need to be able to put your hand into it.

2. Pour lukewarm water into the third bowl. Line these bowls up on the table with the lukewarm water in the middle. Gather an audience. Don't tell them that the water in the bowls differs in temperature. Tell the audience you need their help to determine the temperature of the middle bowl of water.

3. Have a volunteer put one hand in the bowl of cold water. Have a second volunteer put a hand in the bowl of hot water. Tell them to keep their hands in the water for one minute.

4. After one minute, tell them to place the hands that were in the bowls into the middle bowl.

5. Ask them to tell you the temperature of the middle bowl. One will say, "hot," and the other will say, "cold."

How It Works

Your sense of touch is somewhat relative, meaning your brain compares how other things feel to what you are feeling at any given time. For example, let's say you are accustomed to sleeping in a cold bedroom at night. You spend the night at a friend's house where they keep the temperature slightly warmer. It may seem hot to you at their house, when actually it's a moderate temperature. In this trick, the nerve endings in the hand that was in the cold water send a message to the brain that the water feels cold. Over time, the nerve endings adapt and the water doesn't feel as cold as at the beginning. When this hand is placed in lukewarm water, it feels hot because of the drastic temperature change. Likewise, the hand that was in the hot water feels cold when placed in the lukewarm water.

Swimsuit, Sunblock, Ice Axe

Swim in ice-cold water? You must be kidding!? Being able to break the ice and jump in is neither madness nor magic: the science behind enjoying an ice-cold swim is similar to what makes the Hot or Cold? trick on the opposite page work.

Many people choose to swim in the winter for fun and sport. The initial shock of the cold water stimulates a part of the brain to release endorphins, hormones that produce a "feel-good" sensation. The body then adapts to the water and it does not feel as cold. (The same adaptation occurs in Hot or Cold?.)

Cold-water bathers and swimmers could comfortably relax or splash for a long time because they would not notice when their body experienced hypothermia—dangerously low body temperature. To avoid harming themselves, they know not to stay in the water for more than fifteen minutes. (Children have to be extra careful in cold water because they don't have the muscle and fatty tissue of an adult and lose heat more quickly.)

Taking a dip in cold water is not a new idea. The Romans bathed in cold water as a way to cure stomach problems and headaches. Many Scandinavians and other Europeans use cold-water dips in their sauna treatments and claim it increases muscle tone and improves breathing. Members of American and Canadian Polar Bear clubs take an annual chilly dip in a nearby lake or ocean on the first day of each new year.

Ice Fishing

There's no need to fear frostbite when you demonstrate this kind of ice fishing.

What You Need

- Ice cubes
- Plate
- Cup of water
- Cotton string
- Salt

What You Do

1 Place an ice cube on the plate. In this trick you're going to pick up the cube without getting your hands wet.

2 Dip about an inch of the string into the cup of water and place the wet end on top of the ice cube. Sprinkle some salt on top of the string and ice cube. Wait 15 to 20 seconds and then pick up the ice cube with the string.

How It Works

Ice melts at any temperature higher than 32°F—that's its **melting point**. In this trick, the **molecules** of melted ice that result are captured on the surface of the ice and refreeze. The salt you added lowers the ice's melting point. The salt replaces some of the water that would normally refreeze, so the melting happens faster than the freezing. The ice cube absorbs heat from the wet string and the air. As heat is removed from the string, water in the string freezes to the ice cube and you are able to pick it up.

More Fun

Make homemade ice cream using salt! When you mix salt and ice, the concoction melts and creates salty water that has a temperature lower than 32°F. This freezes the ice cream mixture, and you have a tasty treat.

Put 1 tbsp. sugar, ½ cup of milk, and ¼ tsp. of vanilla into a resealable plastic bag and seal it. Place this bag inside a larger resealable plastic bag. Add 2 tablespoons of rock salt and enough ice to fill up the larger bag, and then seal it. Shake, rattle and roll the bag around until the mixture freezes. Yum!

Fireproof!

What You Need

- Adult helper
- 2 balloons
- Water
- Candle lighter

Water balloons are fun to throw, but this trick shows just how cool they really are!

What You Do

1. Fill one of the balloons halfway with water. Then blow it up the rest of the way and tie it off. This works best as a trick if the balloon is not see-through.

2. Blow up the second balloon and tie it off. Carefully hold the balloon without the water over the flame. Be prepared for it to pop. This will show that under normal circumstances a flame will pop a balloon.

3. With an adult nearby, carefully hold the water balloon by the tie and

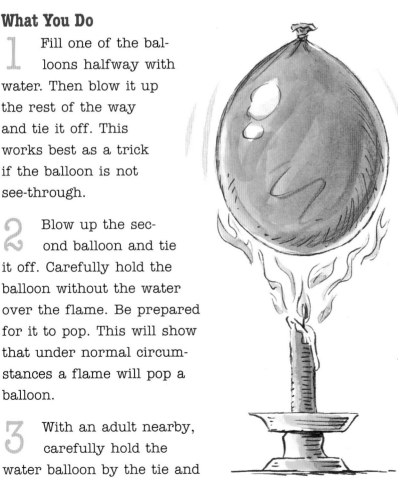

suspend it over the flame. Make sure the bottom part of the balloon that contains the water is over the flame. It won't pop!

How It Works

In the balloon without the water, the intense heat from the flame causes the latex walls of the balloon to weaken. The **pressure** inside the balloon is then so great that it pops. In the water balloon, however, the water conducts the heat away from the latex so that it does not reach a high temperature. The balloon is able to remain inflated as if the flame were not there.

The Precarious Penny

Is it humanly possible to balance a penny on the tip of a coat hanger while you swing it around in a circle? Of course it is.

What You Need

- Wire coat hanger
- Metal file
- Tabletop
- Penny

What You Do

1. File the tip of the hook of the coat hanger so that it creates a small (we're talking very small!), smooth surface for the penny to rest on.

2. Think of the coat hanger as a triangle shape. Grab the horizontal base of the triangle and pull away from the hook. Pull until the coat hanger is in the shape of a diamond.

3. Hold the coat hanger upside down by placing your index finger in the angle at the base of the diamond. Rest the hook on a table. Use your other hand to place the penny on the end of the hook. It should balance.

4. Slowly begin swinging the coat hanger back and forth on your index finger. The penny will stay on the hook.

5. This is impressive, but to really wow an audience, swing the hanger all the way around and upside down. This takes practice, so don't get discouraged.

How It Works

Anything in **motion** wants to go in a straight line unless a **force** acts on it to change it. One of those forces is called **centripetal force**. In this case, the penny ends up going in a circle with the hanger instead of flying off in a straight line (if you swing it fast enough!) As you swing the penny and hanger around, your finger applies force to the hanger in one direction and the hanger and penny apply force in the other. They balance each other out and keep the penny on the hanger.

What Moves You?

Think you know what moves you? Think again! Isaac Newton's three Laws of Motion describe how moving objects behave—including you.

First Law: Something that's not moving will not move unless forced to. Likewise, something in **motion** will continue moving until forced to stop. For instance, you fall asleep—entering a state of **inertia**. Your brother tickles your nose with a feather duster and you sneeze—you've been put in motion. Or, you take a swing and hit a baseball with a bat, sending the ball right at your sister. She snags it with her baseball mitt—stopping the motion.

Second Law: Something in motion will go even faster if a **force** works to move it in the same direction. This is the reasoning behind giving someone a push on a swing or slide. The push—given as you start moving down a slide—accelerates (speeds up) your glide down the slide.

Third Law: To every **action**, there is an equal and opposite **reaction**. This means that there is an interaction between objects anytime anything happens. When you lie on a bed, your mass pushes on the mattress. The mattress' mass pushes up against you, supporting your weight. Use more force and the mattress responds with more force. That's why, when you run and jump on the bed, the mattress doesn't just push up and support you, it bounces you!

Newton did much of this thinking as a teenager growing up on a farm in England in the 1600s. He developed his famous theory of **gravity** by the time he was 23 years old. It says that objects with greater mass attract smaller objects, pulling the smaller objects toward them. Since the Earth is bigger than any object on Earth, everything tends to fall down toward the Earth. Newton spent his life studying and creating mathematical formulas to explain his theories.

Balancing Act

What You Need

- Glass
- Water
- Fork (one that your parents don't mind being a little damaged when you're finished)
- Spoon
- Toothpick
- Match (optional)

What You Do

1 Fill the glass with water. Assemble an audience and explain that you are going to balance the fork, spoon, and toothpick on the glass and then drink the water.

2 Attach the fork and spoon "head to head" by inserting the spoon between the tines of the fork. You'll have to bend the tines of the fork and force the spoon in. The two middle tines should be on the frontside of the spoon. The rest are on the backside of the spoon.

3 Place the toothpick between two of the tines on the fork.

4 Balance the fork and spoon on the rim of the glass of water. This may take some practice. Once you have it balanced, carefully lift the glass of water and take a sip.

5 For more fun, use a match to light the end of the toothpick that is toward the inside of the glass. The toothpick will burn until it reaches the glass and will stay balanced the whole time.

How It Works

When you stand on one foot and lean to one side, you can **balance** as long as your **center of gravity** (or **center of mass**) remains over your foot. This trick works according to the same principle. The fork, spoon, and toothpick balance because the center of mass the whole ensemble is directly below where the toothpick rests on the glass. As long as the center of mass of an object is supported, the object will balance.

One-Buck Bunny Hop

With this trick, gravity wins out over greed!

What You Need
- Volunteer
- Dollar bill

What You Do

1   Place the dollar bill flat on the floor. Ask a volunteer to stand with the dollar bill in front of him. Tell him to bend over and grab his toes.

2   Challenge him to jump over the dollar bill while holding onto his toes (without falling over). Tell him that if he can do it, he can keep the dollar bill. (Don't worry, it's harder than it sounds!)

How It Works

This trick involves using your **center of mass**, or **center of gravity**. This is a point where your body **mass** is concentrated. This trick is virtually impossible to do without losing your **balance** because your center of mass shifts when you try to jump over the dollar bill. Initially, your center of mass is over your feet. When you try to jump, you shift your center of mass forward. Most people need their arms to counterbalance this shift or they lose their balance.

Magic Hand

Combine basic chemistry and sleight of hand in this delightful color-change trick.

What You Need

- Iodine (found with the first-aid supplies at the drug or grocery store)
- Large glass or clear plastic pitcher
- Liquid starch (can be purchased at the grocery store)
- Large jar or bowl (You need to be able to fit your hand inside.)
- Vitamin C tablet

What You Do

1. Assemble your audience. Put a few drops of the iodine into the pitcher. Add water until the solution turns light yellow.

2. Pour the liquid starch into the jar. Dip one of your hands into it. Put your clean hand into the iodine-water solution and stir it around. Nothing will happen. Then put the hand you dipped in starch solution into the pitcher and stir it around. The solution will turn dark blue. Tell your audience this is chemistry at work.

3. Meanwhile, without letting your audience see the vitamin C tablet, pick it up with the hand you placed in the iodine-water solution and hold it between your fingers (in your palm). Put this hand in the solution and stir. Say that magic is more fun than chemistry as the tablet dissolves and the solution turns clear. Don't forget to wash your hands after this trick.

How It Works

This trick works due to chemical **reactions** between the starch and iodine and then the starch-iodine **solution** and vitamin C. The iodine turns the water yellow and is an indicator for starch. When starch is present, the iodine solution will change into a deep blue color. This is because starch contains a **molecule** called amylose that is shaped like a coil. The iodine gets between the coils. This makes the solution blue because the starch-iodine solution absorbs all **wavelengths** of light except blue. When you add the vitamin C tablet it makes the iodine change into iodide (a chemical change) and the solution becomes clear. To turn it back to blue again, you would need to add more starch and iodine until all the vitamin C reacts with the solution.

More is Less

What You Need

- Glass jar with lid
- Water
- Food coloring
- Rubbing alcohol (isopropyl)

What You Do

1. Fill the glass jar three-fourths full with water.

2. Add several drops of food coloring. Put the lid on the jar and mix in the food coloring by gently shaking the jar. This will make the liquid more visible.

3. Slowly add rubbing alcohol to the jar until the jar is full. Be careful not to

shake the jar. Place the lid back on the jar and turn it upside down. Gently shake the jar and then return it to an upright position.

4. Observe the liquid. Some of it has disappeared.

How It Works

Water **molecules** are so small that you can't see them. They're made up of hydrogen and oxygen **atoms** bonded together. The molecules, however, contain large gaps or spaces that other molecules can fit between. This is what happens when substances like salt, sugar, or in this case alcohol mix with water. When the spaces fill, the **volume** of the liquid decreases slightly. This goes against our notion that 1+1=2. In this case 1+1= slightly less than 2.

BOTTOMS UP!

AAAAhh... LESS FILLING!

Tightrope Walking Water

Set this trick up in the evening on a kitchen counter or table and see if your family and friends notice the results in the morning.

What You Need

- 2 glass jars (or a similar see-through container)
- Handkerchief made of silk, linen, or cotton
- Water

What You Do

1   Fill one of the jars with water, and then take the handkerchief and place one end in each jar. Let the jars sit overnight.

2   The more daring water molecules will walk their way from the full jar to the empty one.

How It Works

Water **molecules** have an attraction to other water molecules, which is called **cohesion**, and an attraction to other substances, which is called **adhesion**. This enables something called **capillary action** to occur. The water is pulled up into the spaces in between the fibers in the handkerchief because of cohesion and adhesion. The water soaks up the handkerchief, and then **gravity** pulls it down into the other jar. This continues until the glasses have equal amounts of water.

No-Sip Straws

There's no sleight of hand in this trick—you'll make a perfectly good pair of straws fail with your air pressure know-how.

What You Need

- Volunteer
- Glass
- Water
- 2 straws

What You Do

1 Gather an audience. Pour the glass about three-quarters full of water. Challenge a thirsty member of your audience to drink the water from the glass, following some rules of course.

2 Place one straw inside the glass of water and one straw outside the glass. Ask the volunteer to drink the water by putting both straws in her mouth and sipping. She won't be able to do it.

How It Works

A straw works by using the difference in air **pressure** created between your mouth and the drink. When you pull air into your lungs, the pressure inside the straw is less than the pressure exerted on the water from the atmosphere. Therefore, the water moves up the straw from a high to low pressure. In this trick, as the volunteer tries to "suck up" the water, she's also pulling air from the straw on the outside of the glass. The low pressure needed to pull the water up into the straw is not created, so nothing happens!

58

Waterproof Paper

This paper towel won't soak up any water!

What You Need

- Paper towel
- Small glass
- Water
- Large mixing bowl or saucepan (deep enough to submerge the glass)

What You Do

1. Assemble an audience and tell them that you can put the paper towel underwater without getting it wet. Then crumple up the paper towel and place it in the bottom of the glass.

2. Pour water into the bowl or saucepan until it is about three-quarters full. Turn the glass upside down without the paper towel falling out. You may have to wedge it in the bottom by crumpling it up more.

3. Place the upside-down glass into the bowl of water so that it's submerged. Do not tilt the glass as you do this. Wait a few seconds. Remove the glass by pulling it straight out of the water. Take the paper towel out to show that it's dry.

How It Works

This science trick shows that air takes up space. The air pushes down against the water as the glass is inserted into the bowl. The water is forced around the sides of the opening of the glass and does not fill the glass because air is already there taking up the space. If the glass tilts as you do this, the air has a way to escape and water will fill the glass, wetting the paper towel.

Eye Fooling

Seeing isn't quite as simple as opening your eyes. Complex cooperation between your eyes and your brain makes sight possible. It also makes fooling the eye easy!

To begin with, the pupil must sense light and let it into the eye. (What's a pupil? When you talk about someone's "eye color"—brown, green, blue, etc.—you are talking about the iris. At the center of the iris is a dark circle. That's the pupil.) Then the lens of the eye focuses the light and acts like a movie projector: It shines the light onto the retina, which is sort of like a "screen" in the back of the eye. Its **receptor cells** send millions of messages about the "movie" to the brain. The brain immediately interprets the messages and decides what you are looking at. It determines the color of the images, detects shapes, and even notices the direction of movement. (A blue sky, a flying bird, or even a shadowy figure, if that's all the "light information" the pupil collected.)

Which brings us to **optical illusions**—visual misinterpretations of what is being seen. When you rush to do something, you're more likely to mess it up. The same thing can happen with vision. Optical illusions occur when your brain misinterprets the retina's rapid-fire messages.

In Something Fishy on page 62, you show your audience moving images faster than their brains can process them. That's why the images appear to merge. Our field of vision involves two eyes, and each eye can see something different. That's how you get the illusion of Umm, There's a Hole in Your Hand on the next page. You'll find more optical illusion science tricks on pages 63, 64, and 66.

Umm, There's a Hole in Your Hand

Don't be startled. It's just a science trick.

What You Need

- Paper towel tube

What You Do

1 Look at your hands. Make sure there's not a hole in one of them. Then hold the paper tube up to one of your eyes and look through it at an object in the distance.

2 Hold your other hand up next to the paper tube so that it touches the side of it. Keep both eyes open. What do you see? (It will appear that you have a hole in your hand!)

How It Works

Your brain receives visual information from both of your eyes but merges the signals because it's usually the same field of view. This is called **stereoscopic vision**. In this trick, your brain gets confused because each eye is viewing something different. The two images, one of the distant object and one of your hand, are superimposed (layered) over each other. This makes it appear that you have a hole in your hand!

Something Fishy

What's the secret to this trick? Don't blink!

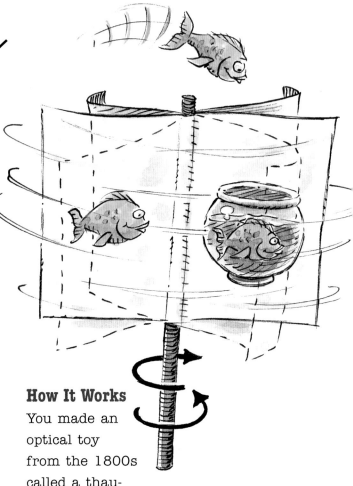

What You Need

- Scissors
- Index card
- Dark colored marker or pen
- Straw
- Clear tape

What You Do

1. Cut the index card in half so that you have two squares. Draw a picture of a fish on one square. Draw a fish bowl on the other. (The bowl should be larger than the fish.)

2. Assemble your audience. Show them each square and tell them that you will put the fish in the bowl using only the straw. Then tape the two pictures back-to-back on the straw.

3. Advise your audience to watch carefully. Quickly twist the straw back and forth between your hands. The fish appears in the bowl!

How It Works

You made an optical toy from the 1800s called a thaumotrope. When you twist the straw back and forth, the images appear to merge and become one. This is because of **persistence of vision**. When you look at an image, it remains on the retina of your eye for about one tenth of a second. If you look at more than ten images per second, your brain combines the images and the scene appears to be moving. Movies take advantage of this phenomenon by showing 24 frames per second, making the images move very smoothly.

Materialize This!

Astonish your audience by making an image appear on a blank page.

What You Need

- Photocopy of image below
- Black marker (optional)
- One piece of 8½ x 11 inch white paper
- Wristwatch or clock with secondhand

What You Do

1 Before you begin you may want to make the image darker with a black marker if the photocopy is too light. Make sure you don't cover the white areas.

2 Gather an audience. Show them both sides of the blank piece of paper. Ask them what they see. (They'll say it's blank.) Act surprised. Tell them there's actually a picture there, but you know a way to help them see it. Set the paper aside.

3 Hold up the photocopy to the audience. Hold it steady. Instruct the audience to stare at the center for at least 30 seconds. (You keep time while they concentrate on the image.)

4 Hold up the blank piece of paper (and put down the photocopy). Ask to audience what they see now. (They'll see a black image. If they have trouble seeing it, have them stare at the photocopy longer.)

How It Works

When you look at the blank white piece of paper you see what's called an **after image**. It's a reverse image of the picture—the areas that were black now look white and the areas that were white look black. This is because staring tires the **receptor cells** in your eye. When you look away, other receptor cells respond and you see the opposite color.

The Spinning Disk

Make colors appear like magic on this spinning disk.

What You Need

- Adult helper
- Old CD (that can be used as scrap)
- Photocopy of disk on page 65
- Scissors
- Glue stick
- Penny
- Pliers
- Candle lighter

What You Do

1. Cut out the photocopy and glue it onto the bottom side of the CD. Make a small slit in the center to fit over the penny.

2. Ask an adult to help you heat the penny over an open flame until hot. (Use the pliers to hold the penny.)

3 Once it's hot, insert the penny into the hole in the middle of the CD so that it is perpendicular to the CD. It should melt the hole in the CD slightly. Hold it in halfway until it cools. What colors do see when the disk is not spinning?

4 Use the penny to spin the CD on a tabletop. You should see colors instead of just the black and white pattern!

How It Works

Toy maker C.E. Benham discovered this and other amazing spinning patterns in 1894. He called his spinning disk an "artificial spectrum top." The reason you see colors is not completely understood. There are several theories, all related to how your eye responds to the alternating black and white patterns. Your eyes have color vision cells called cones. There are three types of cones: some are sensitive to red light, some to green light, and some to blue light. Each type of cone responds at a different rate when stimulated. In this trick, your eye sees flashes of white and black as the CD spins. When you see white, all three types of cones respond. When you see black, the cones begin to turn off. However, they turn on and off at different rates. This difference in reaction times allows you to see different colors.

Quivering Hand

Pick an easy-going friend to perform this trick with—that way she won't be too startled when she sees that her hand is swirling!

What You Need

- Volunteer
- Photocopy of disk (on page 80)
- Scissors
- Pencil or pen
- Cardboard
- Glue stick
- Pushpin
- Toothpick
- Tabletop

What You Do

1. Glue the photocopy of the dotted disk onto the piece of cardboard. Then cut out your disk.

2. Make a hole in the center of the disk with the pushpin. Insert the toothpick through the hole. This is your spinner.

3. Ask a volunteer to stand still and stare at the disk. Spin it on the tabletop for about 10-15 seconds.

4. Now, tell the volunteer to look at her hand. To her, it will appear that her hand is moving!

How It Works

When you stare at something moving, your brain detects the direction of the movement. Your eyes and brain adapt to this movement. Your **receptor cells** become fatigued (tired). When you look away or at another object, other receptor cells that respond to movement in the opposite direction are stimulated. This is called the **motion after effect** or **waterfall effect**.

Magic Cloth

Your audience will say this trick is real magic because the science is unbelievable.

What You Need

- Adult helper
- Large coin
- Cotton handkerchief
- Candle lighter

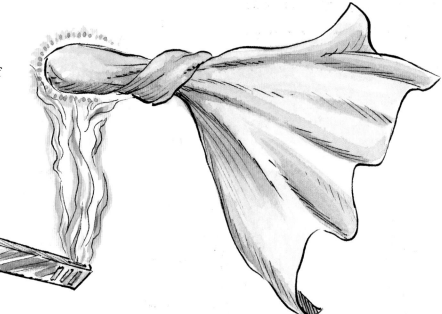

What You Do

1. Place the coin in the middle of the handkerchief. Wrap the cloth around the coin and hold it together so that the coin is tightly covered.

2. Gather an audience and tell them you can put a flame to a normal handkerchief without causing it to burn.

3. Using the candle lighter, hold the cloth-covered coin over the flame. Be careful not to get the flame close to your hands. The cloth will not burn. If your audience simply thinks you have a piece of fireproof fabric, repeat the demonstration with a coin wrapped in a piece of paper. That will show them!

How It Works

The metal in the coin is a good **conductor** of heat. The cloth doesn't reach a temperature high enough to ignite because the coin conducts the heat away from it.

How Houdini Did It

Have you heard of Harry Houdini? He was a **physicist** and **engineer** who invented lots of gadgets. He did magic too.

Most people only know the magic part—his amazing escapes. But science know-how helped Houdini become the world's most famous escape artist. (An escape artist is someone who specializes in freeing himself from ropes, chains, handcuffs, boxes, and just about anything else you can use to confine him.)

Houdini spent years working out each trick and inventing the gimmicks and props he needed. A **gimmick** is a secret device used to do a magic trick. (The hole in the bottle on Light-headed on page 24 is a gimmick.) A **prop** is anything magicians use to assist them in their show. (In Balloon Kebabs on page 30, the balloon and the skewers are props.)

Houdini's most famous trick was the Water Torture Cell. The cell looked like a cross between an aquarium and a casket. Houdini locked himself in chains and padlocks, and then locked his feet to the inside lid of the cell. He asked the audience to take a deep breath with him, and then he was dunked into the cell—upside down. Assistants pulled a curtain around the cell. After several minutes—much longer than a person could hold his breath—Houdini emerged from the cell, wet but alive.

How did he do it? The tank was a gimmick—it wasn't really full of water. A band of metal at the top hid an air pocket. Houdini was althletic and flexible; he bent over and breathed easy as he opened the chains and locks. (Did you guess that he made the locks himself? Houdini was also a master locksmith.)

Disappearing Water

Make ordinary water disappear with a quick sleight of hand and an amazing ingredient.

What You Need

- Moisture-saving pellets (sold at local hardware store or plant nursery)
- Measuring spoon
- Measuring cups
- 2 plastic cups (not clear)
- Pitcher of water
- Table salt

What You Do

1. Before you ask anyone to watch you, measure and pour 1 tablespoon of the pellets into the plastic cup. Fill the pitcher with water.

2. Tell your audience that you can make the water in the pitcher disappear.

3. Pour about ¼ cup of water into the cup. Ask your audience to agree that it was plain water that splashed into the cup, and that it certainly would be amazing if that water disappeared. Meanwhile, the liquid will transform into a mass that sticks to the sides and bottom of the cup. Show the audience that the water is gone by turning the cup upside down. (Don't let them look in the cup.)

4. Tell the audience that with any luck you can get the water to reappear. Add some table salt to the cup—saying that a sprinkle of salt is good luck—and stir.

5. Pour the water from the first cup into the second cup. Act surprised!

How It Works

Moisture-saving pellets contain a **polymer** called sodium polyacrylate. It's similar to the polymers in disposable diapers and acts like a sponge. As it **absorbs** moisture, the polymer expands and turns into a semi-solid gel. Table salt **reacts** with the gel, releasing the water to its liquid state.

Electrified Fruit

> Create a contraption that delivers a gentle jolt.

What You Need

- Adult helper
- Volunteer
- 18-gauge copper wire
- Pliers
- Wire cutters
- Steel paper clip
- Coarse sandpaper
- Lemon

What to Do

1. Have an adult strip 2 inches of insulation off the copper wire. (The insulation is the covering.) Snip off the 2 inches of exposed wire with the clippers.

2. Straighten the paper clip and cut off about a 2-inch length. Sand the ends of the wire and paper clip.

3. Squeeze the lemon or roll it on a table to soften the insides without breaking the skin. Push the copper wire into the lemon, and then push the 2-inch section of paper clip into the lemon so that they are side by side but not touching. Have a volunteer moisten her tongue, and then touch it to both ends of the wires. She'll get a shock.

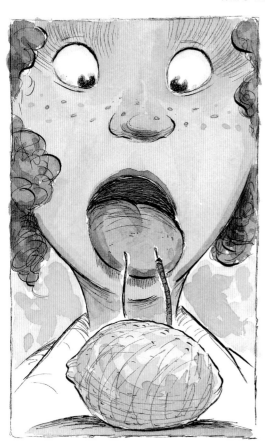

How It Works

Electricity is the flow of tiny **particles** called **electrons** in an **atom**. Materials called **conductors** allow the electrons to flow through them. A **battery** stores electrical energy. A battery is made up of two different metals bathed in an acidic solution or powder. The steel paper clip and the copper wire are the conductors in this battery. The lemon juice is the acidic solution, also called an **electrolyte**. One metal has a positive **charge** and one has a negative charge. When you place your tongue on the metals, you complete the **circuit** and create an electrical **current**, as electrons go from the negatively charged metal through your tongue to the positively charged metal, through the lemon juice, and back around again and again.

Tough Tissue

The surprise is that there's no hoax here— just one tough tissue.

What You Need

- Facial tissue or tissue paper
- Empty paper towel tube
- Rubber band
- Rice
- Broom handle or dowel

What You Do

1 Place a piece of tissue over one end of the paper towel tube. Carefully secure it with the rubber band. Rest the end of the tube with the tissue on a table. Fill the tube about three-quarters full with rice.

2 Holding the tube off the table, push as hard as you can inside the tube with the broom handle. No matter how hard you try, you won't be able to rip the tissue.

How It Works

As the rice fills the paper towel tube, pockets of air become trapped between the pieces of rice. When you push down with the broom handle, the air spaces become smaller, and the rice grains move closer. The rice absorbs the **pressure** and the tissue does not tear.

FireStarter Fingers

Make smoke in a snap and set a dark room aglow with fantastic phosphorous fingertips.

What You Need

- Adult helper
- A dark room
- Book of paper matches with cardboard cover
- Metal pan
- Scorch-proof work surface
- Extra matchbook or lighter

What You Do

1. Tear the scratchy flint strip from the matchbook. Set aside the rest of the matchbook. Place the flint strip with the cardboard side up in the pan.

2. Have the adult light the strip with the extra matchbook or lighter. Let the strip burn out.

3. After the pan has cooled, rub the tip of your index finger and thumb in the residue in the pan. Rub them together to see your fingers smoke. Turn out the light and your fingertips will glow!

How It Works

The striking surface on a match book contains a chemical called red phosphorus. As it burns some of it **condenses** on the surface of the metal pan as white phosphorus. It is reactive with oxygen in the air. When you put the residue on your fingers and rub them together, the phosphorus slowly **reacts** with the oxygen, creating a greenish glow.

Money Grabber

This trick is like a good carnival game: it looks easy until you try it!

What You Need

- Volunteer
- Dollar bill
- Tabletop

What You Do

1 Assemble an audience. Present your dollar bill and tell them that if a volunteer can catch it—your way— he or she can keep it.

2 Ask a volunteer to place her arm on a tabletop with her hand over the edge. Make sure her wrist is on the table. Have her open her hand.

3 Hold the bill by the top edge and place it between her thumb and fingers. The fingers should be right at the middle of the bill. Make sure her fingers are not touching the bill at all.

4 Tell your volunteer to watch the bill carefully, and then without warning, drop the bill.

5 She won't be able to catch the bill. Try it again, or call on another volunteer. Vary when you let the bill go, and talk to your volunteer before letting the bill go in order to keep her distracted.

How It Works

When the volunteer's eyes see the bill drop, that information travels to her brain, which then sends a "grab it" signal to the muscles in her hand. This takes less than half a second. But **gravity** is a little faster. You can do this trick without putting the volunteer's arm on the table, but at some point volunteers might get smart and start moving their hands downward to catch the bill. (If they do that, it's easy to catch the dollar bill.)

Perfectly Peculiar Paper Rings

Can your audience deduce which paper strip will produce an endlessly twisting ring?

What You Need

- 8½ x 11-inch piece of paper
- Scissors
- Tape
- Pen or pencil

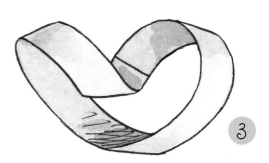

What You Do

1. Show a piece of paper to your audience. Explain that you'll create a ring from it that has only one side and one edge.

2. Cut three strips from the paper, measuring approximately 1 inch wide and 11 inches long.

3. Get three volunteers. Have them make three rings of paper as follows: one with no twist in the end (see illustration 1); one with a half twist in one end (see illustration 2); and one with a full twist in one end (see illustration 3). Have each volunteer tape the ends of his ring together to create three separate rings that resemble those drawn here.

4 Have each volunteer draw a line down the middle of his strip. Notice that each ring has a line that goes all the way around and back to its beginning—even the twisted strips. Ask each volunteer to cut along his line. (See illustration 4.) Your audience will see the surprising results.

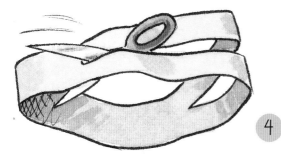

The first one will yield two rings (see illustration 5), as you might expect. The second yields a large, endlessly twisting ring (see illustration 6). The third (see illustration 7) will yield two interlocking, endlessly twisting rings!

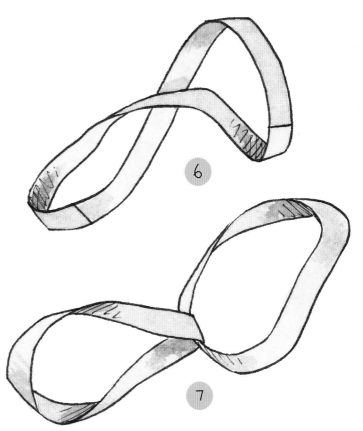

How It Works

Astronomer and mathematician August Ferdinand Möbius invented these endlessly twisting paper rings while studying a branch of mathematics called topology. Topology is the study of geometric shapes that do not change when they are stretched or bent. Moebius strips are used in making filmstrips and conveyor belts because they last longer and get more use. With only one side, they wear equally. Magicians have been using the Moebius strip in their bag of tricks since the 1880s!

Hopping Dice

What You Need

- Volunteer
- 2 dice or game pieces
- Mug or plastic cup

The laws of motion are your secret weapons as you alone can handle hopping dice.

What You Do

1. Ask a volunteer to try to catch a die in the cup. First, he holds a die against the side of the cup in one hand, then throws it up and catches it in the cup.

2. Tell him he made it look easy, and then challenge him to repeat step one with the second die while leaving the first die in the cup. When he tries, the second one goes in, but the first one pops out.

3. Have several volunteers try. A lucky few might get it, but most likely they will not. After several attempts by your volunteers, show them how it's done. After you've caught the first die, get ready to catch the second, but instead of jerking the cup upward, jerk the cup downward. You'll easily catch the second die without displacing the first one.

How It Works

When your volunteers try to catch the second die, they're working against **gravity** by jerking the cup upward. The force of the upward **motion** is greater than the pull of gravity on the die, so the first die flies out. When you move the cup downward instead of upward, you are working with gravity, which means that the first die will stay in the cup as you catch the second one.

Take a Bow!

The show's over for us, but we hope your
fun with this book has just begun.
May your every performance dazzle
and astound. Stay Amazing, Great,
and Splendiferous.

—Tim, Jessie, and Lucinda

P.S. If you dug this book, you'll love
**Chemistry Concoctions:
50 Formulas that Fizz, Foam, Splatter & Ooze!**,
in which we turn Lucinda's garage
into a chemistry lab!

Glossary

Absorb. To soak up or take in a substance

Adhesion. The physical attraction or joining of two substances

Action. To do something; any use of energy

After image. Optical illusion in which the eyes see a reverse image. Colors appear as their opposite in the color spectrum

Atom. A unit of matter; the smallest unit of an element

Balance. A state of equilibrium

Battery. Two or more connected cells that produce a current by converting chemical energy to electrical energy

Bernoulli effect. When the speed of a fluid (water, air, oil, etc.) increases, its pressure decreases

Bernoulli principle. *See* Bernoulli effect

Capillary action. The movement of water within the spaces of a porous material due to the forces of adhesion and cohesion. Also called capillary effect

Center of gravity. An imaginary point where an object's weight is concentrated; same as center of mass, if gravity is uniform

Center of mass. *See* Center of gravity

Centripetal force. What causes an object to move in a circle, directing it towards the center of the circle

Charge. A measure, either positive or negative, of the force of electromagnetic interaction between matter

Circuit. A closed path followed or capable of being followed by an electrical current

Cohesion. Molecules sticking together

Compress. To press together or make more compact

Condense. To lose heat and change from a vapor into a liquid or solid

Conductor. A substance through which electrical charges or heat can easily flow

Conjurer. Someone who performs tricks involving sleight of hand and the illusion of magic as entertainment; someone believed to practice magic or conjure supernatural forces

Contract. To reduce in size by drawing together or shrinking

Convection. The transfer of heat in a gas or liquid by the circulation of currents from one region to another

Current. A flow of electrical charge

Dense. Thick or highly concentrated

Effort. Mental or physical energy or exertion

Electrolyte. Chemical compound that conducts electricity from one electrode to the other inside a fuel cell such as a battery

Electron. A particle of the atom having a negative electrical charge

Energy. The ability to do work or activity

Engineer. Someone who applies scientific and mathematical principles to practical ends such as the design, manufacture, and operation of machines, processes, and systems

Expand. To increase in size, volume, or quantity

Fakir. A member of an Eastern religious order; a person who performs feats of magic or endurance

Fluid. Anything that flows, including gases, oil, and water

Force. A push or pull that gives energy to an object

Friction. Resistance between moving objects

Fulcrum. The point or support on which a lever rotates

Gimmick. A device or a scheme used to deceive or trick

Gravity. The natural force of attraction exerted by Earth upon objects that tends to draw them toward the center of the mass

Inertia. The tendency of a body to remain at rest or in uniform motion unless acted on by an outside force

Inflate. To fill something with air or gas so as to make it swell

Laws of motion. The three laws proposed by Isaac Newton to define the concept of a force and describe motion

Lever. A simple machine consisting of a rigid bar pivoted (rotated) on a fixed point and used to transmit force, as in raising or moving a weight at one end by pushing down on the other

Mass. A unified body of matter with no specific shape

Melt. To dissolve or change from a solid to a liquid

Melting point. The temperature at which a solid becomes a liquid

Misdirect. To purposely mislead or confuse. Magicians misdirect their audiences to hide the science behind their tricks

Molecule. The smallest particle of a substance, usually composed of two or more atoms

Motion. The act or process of changing position or place

Motion after effect. When a person stares at movement in a particular direction for a short time, then looks at something that's not moving, causing the unmoving scene to appear to move in the opposite direction

Optical illusions. Visual misinterpretations of what is being seen

Particle. A very small portion of matter

Patter. Talk that's meant to entertain and take someone's mind off something

Persistence of vision. A phenomenon in which the human eye retains an image for a split second or longer

Physical feat. A bodily act of skill or imagination

Physicist. A scientist who specializes in the study of matter and energy and the interaction between the two

Polymers. Natural or synthetic (man-made) compounds consisting of large molecules made up of many chemically bonded smaller identical molecules. Starch and nylon are polymers

Pressure. Force applied to or distributed over a surface

Prop. An item used in a performance to assist the performer

Reaction. A response to an action or substance

Reacts. Responds to a substance or action

Receptor cells. Specialized group of nerve endings that respond to light, heat, and other sensory stimuli

Rest. The absence of motion; still, quiet, or inactive

Seal. A closure that prevents the entry or exit of air, water, or other substances

Showmanship. Having a flair for dramatic behavior

Sleight of hand. A trick or action performed so quickly that the way it's done can't be figured out

Solution. A material made up of two or more substances mixed together uniformly

Sound waves. The energy produced by a sound, which moves outward as a wave in all directions and is carried by a solid, liquid or gas

Stereoscopic vision. A three-dimensional effect caused when viewing two images of the same scene at slightly different angles

Strands. The material in woven or braided substance

Vibrate. To move back and forth or to and fro, especially rhythmically and rapidly

Volume. The amount of space occupied by a liquid, solid, or gas

Vortex. A whirling mass of water or air

Vortex generator. A mechanism that causes a whirling mass of water or air, and draws everything toward its center; used on aircraft to help speed up air flowing over the wings

Waterfall effect. *See* Motion after effect

Wavelength. A segment of a wave of light, heat, or other energy

Template
Quivering Hand on page 66

Enlarge 200%

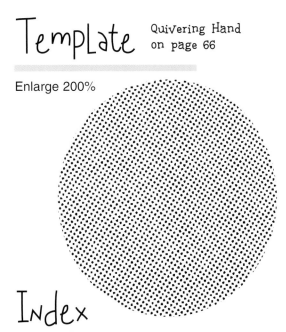

Metric Conversions

To convert degrees Fahrenheit to degrees Celsius, subtract 32 and then multiply by .56.
To convert inches to centimeters, multiply by 2.5.
To convert ounces to grams, multiply by 28.
To convert teaspoons to milliliters, multiply by 5.
To convert tablespoons to milliliters, multiply by 15.
To convert fluid ounces to milliliters, multiply by 30.
To convert cups to liters, multiply by .24.

Index

AUG   2005